Granddaddy Leonard Frett
TO
All 6 of your Grandkids
Ty, Nazir, Luck, Mariah, Nadia and
FROM   Z' Niyah

March 29, 2018
DATE
We love You!

It is not what he has, nor what he does,
which directly expresses the worth of a man,
but what he is.

HENRI-FREDERIC AMIEL

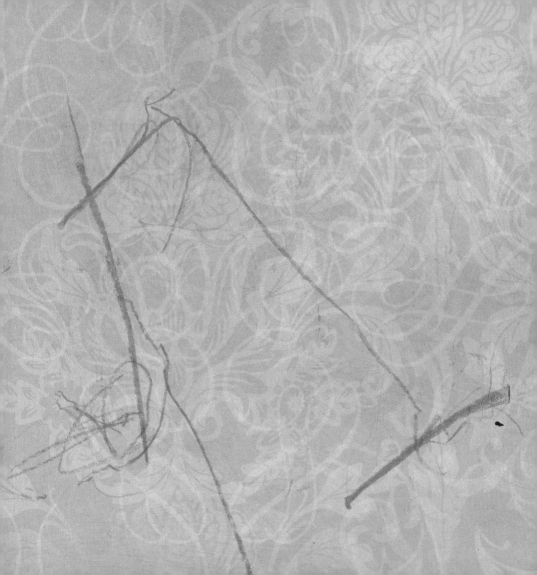

You're One Amazing Grandpa

ARTWORK BY

Lori Siebert

HARVEST HOUSE PUBLISHERS
EUGENE, OREGON

You're One Amazing Grandpa

Artwork copyright © by Olika Licensing, inc./Lori Siebert
Text copyright © 2013 by Harvest House Publishers

Published by Harvest House Publishers
Eugene, Oregon 97402
www.harvesthousepublishers.com

ISBN 978-0-7369-4515-8

Design and production by Garborg Design Works, Savage, Minnesota

Harvest House Publishers has made every effort to trace the ownership of all poems and quotes. In the event of a question arising from the use of a poem or quote, we regret any error made and will be pleased to make the necessary correction in future editions of this book.

All Scripture quotations are taken from The Holy Bible, New International Version® NIV®. Copyright © 1973, 1978, 1984, 2011, by Biblica, Inc.™ Used by permission of Zondervan. All rights reserved worldwide. www.zondervan.com

Printed in China

13 14 15 16 17 18 19 / FC / 10 9 8 7 6 5 4 3 2 1

There is no grandfather who does not adore his grandson.

VICTOR HUGO

YOU HAVE TO DO YOUR
OWN GROWING NO
MATTER HOW TALL YOUR
GRANDFATHER WAS.

IRISH PROVERB

It is a fine thing to have ability,
but the ability to discover ability
in others is the true test.

ELBERT HUBBARD

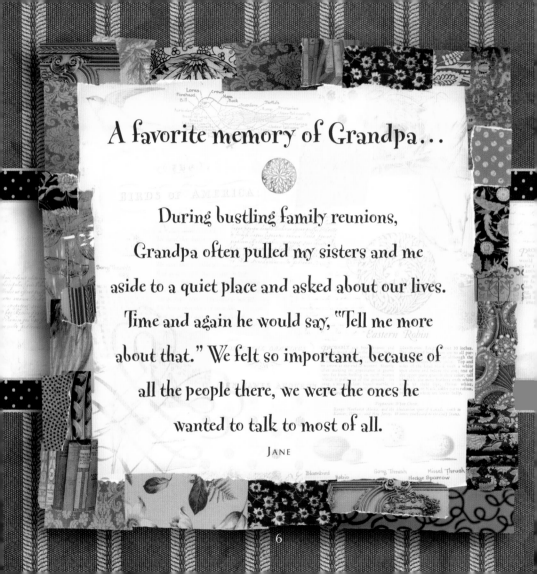

A favorite memory of Grandpa…

During bustling family reunions,
Grandpa often pulled my sisters and me
aside to a quiet place and asked about our lives.
Time and again he would say, "Tell me more
about that." We felt so important, because of
all the people there, we were the ones he
wanted to talk to most of all.

JANE

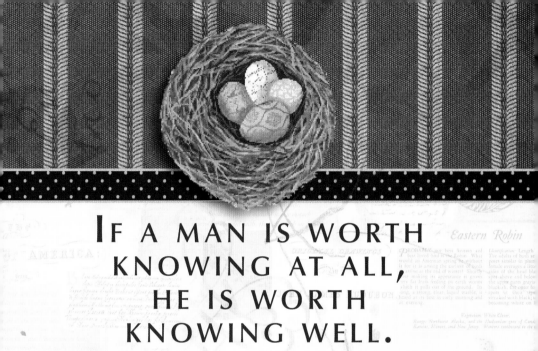

IF A MAN IS WORTH KNOWING AT ALL, HE IS WORTH KNOWING WELL.

ALEXANDER SMITH

Grandpa's hugs are the

biggest and the best!

To forget one's ancestors is to
be a brook without a source,
a tree without a root.

CHINESE PROVERB

The best portion of a good man's life is his little, nameless, unremembered acts of kindness and of love.

WILLIAM WORDSWORTH

Those who loved you and were helped by you will remember you when forget-me-nots have withered. Carve your name on hearts, not on marble.

CHARLES H. SPURGEON

FOND
MEMORY
BRINGS
THE LIGHT
OF OTHER DAYS
AROUND ME:
THE SMILES,
THE TEARS
OF BOYHOOD'S
YEARS.

THOMAS MOORE

12

A favorite memory of Poppa...

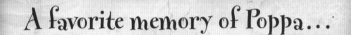

My poppa loved adventure and a good challenge. While on a mountain hike to pick huckleberries with the family, Poppa hiked out in front of the group. As we rounded the corner to catch up with him, we were stunned to see Poppa precariously balancing on his head—on the top of a rock ledge!

SUE

We live in deeds, not years;
in thoughts, not breaths; in
feelings, not in figures on the
dial; we should count time by
heart-throbs. He most lives
who thinks most, feels the
noblest, acts the best.

PHILIP JAMES BAILEY

I love Grandpa,

and Grandpa loves me.

OUR HOME JOYS ARE THE MOST
DELIGHTFUL EARTH AFFORDS,
AND THE JOY OF PARENTS IN
THEIR CHILDREN IS THE MOST
HOLY JOY OF HUMANITY. IT
MAKES THEIR HEARTS PURE AND
GOOD, IT LIFTS MEN UP TO THEIR
FATHER IN HEAVEN.

JOHANN H. PESTALOZZI

Be such a man, and live such a life, that if every man were such as you, and every life a life like yours, this earth would be God's Paradise.

PHILLIPS BROOKS

A favorite memory of Granddad…

When I stayed at Granddad's house, I would wake up early and quietly sneak up the stairs to join Granddad in the kitchen, right where I knew he would be. As I climbed onto my oversized stool at the counter next to him, he would butter my toast and pour a bowl of cereal for me so we could eat breakfast together and talk about everything that was important to us.

DAN

AN AGED
CHRISTIAN,
WITH THE SNOW
OF TIME ON
HIS HEAD, MAY
REMIND US
THAT THOSE
POINTS OF
EARTH ARE THE
WHITEST WHICH
ARE NEAREST
HEAVEN.

EDWIN HUBBEL CHAPIN

I hope I grow up to be as

smart as Grandpa.

But every house where Love abides,
And friendship is a guest,
Is surely home, and home-sweet-home:
For there the heart can rest.

HENRY VAN DYKE

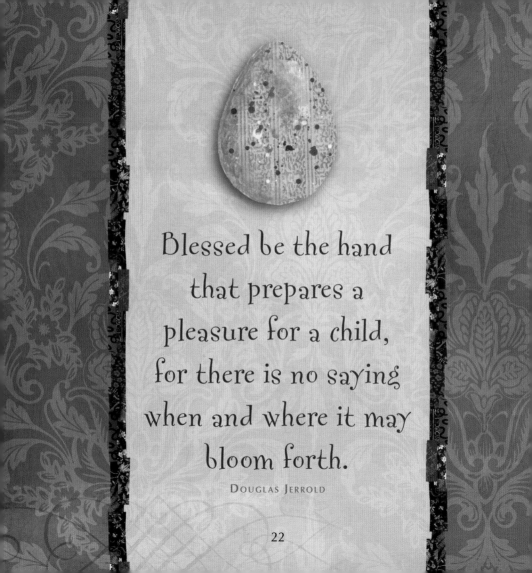

Blessed be the hand
that prepares a
pleasure for a child,
for there is no saying
when and where it may
bloom forth.

DOUGLAS JERROLD

NEVER FEAR
SPOILING
CHILDREN BY
MAKING THEM
TOO HAPPY.
HAPPINESS
IS THE
ATMOSPHERE
IN WHICH
ALL GOOD
AFFECTIONS
GROW.

THOMAS BRAY

Good-nature is the very air of a
good mind; the sign of a large and
generous soul, and the peculiar soil
in which virtue prospers.

GODFREY GOODMAN

A favorite memory of Grandpa...

Grandpa used to take me outside to see his garden. There he would find just the right rose—not too open, not too closed, and with the sweetest fragrance—nip it off with his pocketknife, and give it to me. Every time he did this, I knew that he had given me one of his treasures... and it made me feel special.

ANNA

Grandpa takes time to

THERE IS
ONLY ONE
HAPPINESS
IN LIFE, TO
LOVE AND
BE LOVED.

GEORGE SAND

answer all my questions.

Your actions, in passing,
pass not away, for every
good work is a grain of seed
for eternal life.

SAINT BERNARD OF CLAIRVAUX

A kind heart is a fountain of
gladness, making everything in its
vicinity to freshen into smiles.

WASHINGTON IRVING

A favorite memory of Gramps…

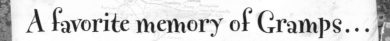

Gramps loved to tell jokes and
would laugh loud and long at
the end of each one.
I didn't always get them,
but when he laughed,
it made me laugh too.

WILLIAM

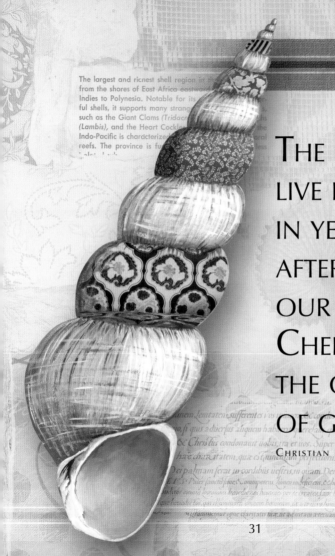

The largest and richest shell region in the
from the shores of East Africa eastward
Indies to Polynesia. Notable for its
ful shells, it supports many strang
such as the Giant Clams (Tridac
(Lambis), and the Heart Cock
Indo-Pacific is characterize
reefs. The province is fu

THE CHEERFUL
LIVE LONGEST
IN YEARS, AND
AFTERWARDS IN
OUR REGARDS.
CHEERFULNESS IS
THE OFF-SHOOT
OF GOODNESS.

CHRISTIAN NESTELL BOVEE

My grandpa makes

You will find as you look back
upon life that the moments
when you have really lived are
the moments when you have
done things in the spirit of love.

HENRY DRUMMOND

me feel special.

CHILDREN'S CHILDREN ARE

A CROWN TO THE AGED,

AND PARENTS ARE THE

PRIDE OF THEIR CHILDREN.

THE BOOK OF PROVERBS

Don't judge each day by the harvest you reap, but by the seeds you plant.

ROBERT LOUIS STEVENSON

PERFECT LOVE
SOMETIMES DOES
NOT COME TILL THE
FIRST GRANDCHILD.

WELSH PROVERB

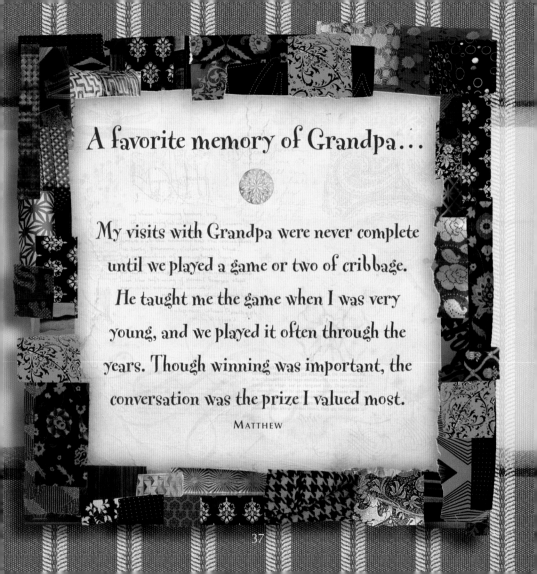

A favorite memory of Grandpa…

My visits with Grandpa were never complete until we played a game or two of cribbage. He taught me the game when I was very young, and we played it often through the years. Though winning was important, the conversation was the prize I valued most.

MATTHEW

I love to hear
Grandpa's
stories about the
good ol' days.

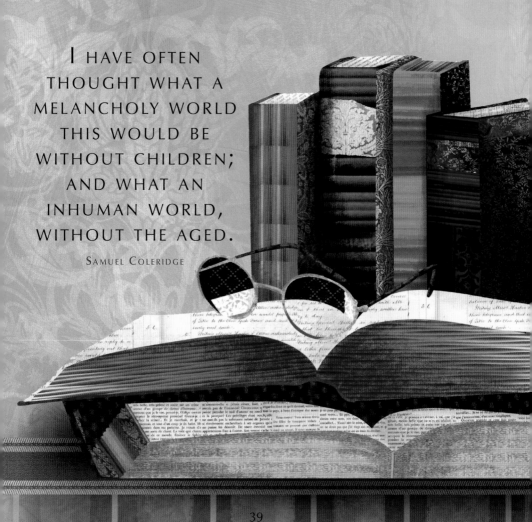

I HAVE OFTEN
THOUGHT WHAT A
MELANCHOLY WORLD
THIS WOULD BE
WITHOUT CHILDREN;
AND WHAT AN
INHUMAN WORLD,
WITHOUT THE AGED.

SAMUEL COLERIDGE

WHAT IS STRENGTH WITHOUT A DOUBLE SHARE OF WISDOM?

JOHN MILTON

The heart of a good man is the sanctuary of God in this world.

MADAME NECKER

A favorite memory of Granddad...

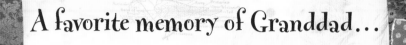

Though my granddad lived two states away,
he was faithful to attend the important
events of my life. Often he took the bus.
Sometimes he even drove all that way
by himself. No matter how he got there,
he made sure I knew that he was
my biggest fan.

PEGGY

The creed of the true
saint is to make the
most of life, and
to make the
best of it.

EDWIN HUBBEL CHAPIN

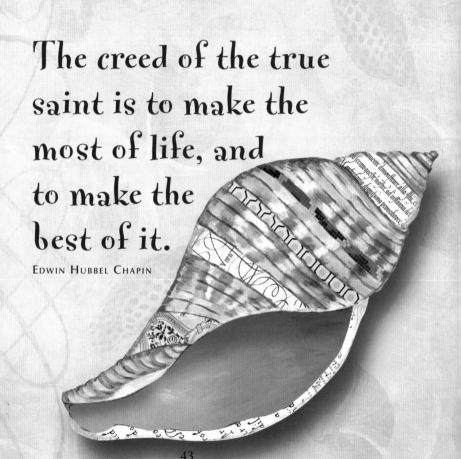

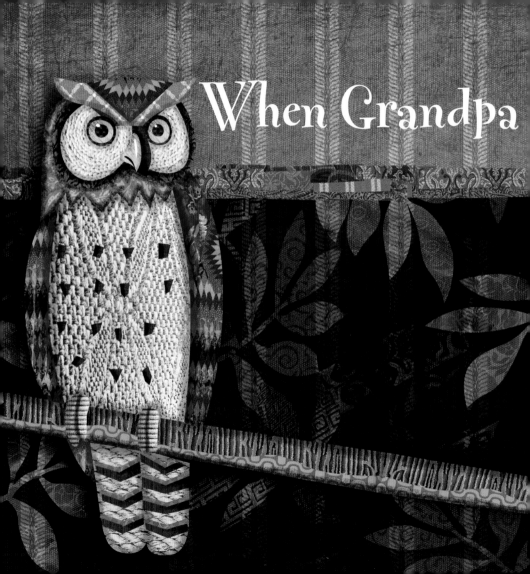

When Grandpa

laughs, his eyes twinkle.

The training of children is a
profession, where we must
know how to lose time in
order to gain it.

JEAN-JACQUES ROUSSEAU

To make knowledge valuable, you must have the cheerfulness of wisdom. Goodness smiles to the last.

RALPH WALDO EMERSON

A man cannot leave a better legacy to the world than a well-educated family.

THOMAS SCOTT

Show me your ways, LORD,
teach me your paths.
Guide me in your truth and teach me.

THE BOOK OF PSALMS

A favorite memory of Pops...

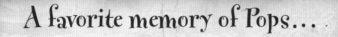

When Pops volunteered to tell the bedtime
story, my brother and sister and I actually
hurried to get ready for bed. His stories were
magical and suspenseful. He spun tales about
wild adventures in faraway lands and people
who seemed uncannily familiar and reacted in
ways we would. It was great fun to listen and
disappear within the storyline.

DOUG

HIS DAILY PRAYER, FAR
BETTER UNDERSTOOD IN
ACTS THAN IN WORDS,
WAS SIMPLY DOING
GOOD.

JOHN GREENLEAF WHITTIER

Grandpa's heart is as big

as the whole wide world!

LET US NEVER
FORGET THAT EVERY
STATION IN LIFE IS
NECESSARY; THAT
EACH DESERVES OUR
RESPECT, THAT NOT
THE STATION ITSELF,
BUT THE WORTHY
FULFILLMENT OF ITS
DUTIES DOES HONOR
TO THE MAN.

MARY LYON

*Like a morning dream, life
becomes more and more bright
the longer we live, and the reason
of everything appears more clear.
What has puzzled us before seems
less mysterious, and the crooked
paths look straighter as we
approach the end.*

JEAN PAUL RICHTER

A favorite memory of Gramps…

As soon as I was old enough to hold a pole,
Gramps taught me to fish. Through the years,
we went to our favorite fishing holes as often
as we could. Between baiting our hooks,
casting our lines, and reeling in the big ones,
he shared his wisdom with me as I shared
my youth with him.

TIM

Hereditary honors are a noble and splendid treasure to descendants.

PLATO

Grandpa makes every

day a special day.

THERE NEVER WAS ANY HEART

TRULY GREAT AND GRACIOUS

THAT WAS NOT ALSO TENDER

AND COMPASSIONATE.

ROBERT SOUTH

For the LORD is good
and his love endures forever;
his faithfulness continues
through all generations.

THE BOOK OF PSALMS

NO LONGER FORWARD NOR BEHIND
I LOOK IN HOPE OR FEAR;
BUT, GRATEFUL, TAKE THE GOOD I FIND,
THE BEST OF NOW AND HERE.

JOHN GREENLEAF WHITTIER

Show me the man you honor, and I will
know what kind of a man you are, for it
shows me what your ideal of manhood is,
and what kind of a man you long to be.

THOMAS CARLYLE

60

I THINK THAT TO HAVE KNOWN
ONE GOOD, OLD MAN—ONE
MAN, WHO, THROUGH THE
CHANCES AND MISCHANCES
OF A LONG LIFE, HAS CARRIED
HIS HEART IN HIS HAND, LIKE
A PALM-BRANCH, WAVING
ALL DISCORDS INTO PEACE—
HELPS OUR FAITH IN GOD, IN
OURSELVES, AND IN EACH OTHER
MORE THAN MANY SERMONS.

GEORGE WILLIAM CURTIS

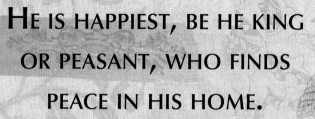

He is happiest, be he king
or peasant, who finds
peace in his home.

GOETHE

Grandpa is my hero.

The largest and richest shell region in the world extends from the shores of East Africa eastward through the East Indies to Polynesia. Notable for its abundance of colorful shells, it supports many strange and unique mollusks, such as the Giant Clam (Tridacna), the Scorpion Conch (Lambis), and the Spider Conch. The Indo-Pacific is also noted for its coral reefs. The pr...

ecendit. Ipse est chri...
rinum se cognoscit. Non...
tu noueris emendare del...
n. Dei destruit meliore...

Dost thou love life? Then do not squander time, for that is the stuff life is made of.

BENJAMIN FRANKLIN

Imodum & Christus condonauit uobis, ita et uos. Super.
m omnia hæc charitatem, quæ est uinculum perfectionis
t pax Dei palmam ferat in cordibus uestris, in quam Dei
une D E I S Pater sanctissime, omnipotens, lumen indeficiens, & be-
ime Conditor omnii humium, benedic nos homines per te creatos, sanc ti
tos atque benedic tos, qui illuminasti omnem hominem, ut a te uero lumi
cens   na hamminemur igne claritatis tuæ, ut ad uitam æternam.
Christum d...

63

*It is the man that dignifies
the calling. Nothing that is
necessary to be done is small
when a great soul does it.*

ORISON SWETT MARDEN